CURRENTLY TRENDING:
2025 WEEK 1

CURRENTLY TRENDING: 2025 WEEK 1
© 2025 Critical Blast Publishing. All Rights Reserved.

Critical Blast Publishing, 24 Hillside Drive Suite A, Holiday Island, AR 72631

Book Design, Title Logo, Typesetting by George Peter Gatsis.   GeorgePeterGatiss•com

First Edition January 2025

0 9 8 7 6 5 4 3 2 1

ISBN: 978-1-998564-51-4   (Digest Edition)

The content is satire and humor. It may contain exaggerated, fictionalized, or otherwise inaccurate information. Interpret the content with an understanding that it is not meant to be taken as a factual representation of events, people, or situations. Enjoy responsibly.

Any similarities between the characters, names, persons, and/or institutions in this book and any living, dead or fictional characters, names, persons and/or institutions is not intended and it exists purely coincidental.

Distributed by Critical Blast Logistics - CriticalBlast.com / PRINTED IN USA.

CONTENTS

1. Celebrities and Brands on Threads

Threads, Meta's new social media platform, has strategically launched with an impressive lineup of celebrities and brands to drive user engagement from day one. Names like Netflix, Gordon Ramsay, and Michael Strahan were among the first to join, leveraging their massive followings to bring attention to the app. This move was seen as a tactical play to quickly establish a user base and compete with existing platforms like X, by providing instant credibility and content.

The effect of this celebrity endorsement was immediate, with millions signing up in the first few hours post-launch. This not only helped in showcasing the platform's potential but also set a precedent for how social media platforms could potentially launch in the future. The presence of high-profile figures has led to a diverse range of content, from personal anecdotes to brand promotions, creating a vibrant ecosystem that's appealing to a wide demographic.

However, this strategy also raises questions about the authenticity of social media interactions when platforms are seeded with influencers from the get-go. While it has provided Threads with a significant boost, there's an ongoing debate about whether this approach will maintain long-term user engagement or if it's merely a short-term popularity spike. The move has certainly put Threads on the map, but only time will tell if it can sustain interest without continuously relying on celebrity power.

And remember, with all these celebrities on Threads, it's like they're trying to make the platform the new Hollywood Walk of Fame, but instead of stars on the ground, we get influencers in our feeds. Why did the celebrity join Threads? Because they heard it was the latest trend to "thread" their fame!

2. Threads Launches Trending Topics

Threads has now introduced a feature that many social media users are familiar with: trending topics. This functionality, initially rolled out to U.S. users, allows Threads to show what's currently capturing the public's interest in real-time, much like X does. This addition is aimed at enhancing user experience by providing a pulse on what's happening globally or within specific communities on the platform.

The implementation of trending topics has sparked various discussions, including political ones, despite Meta's initial reluctance to delve into politics. Topics like Trump's legal proceedings have made it onto the trending list, showing that even with a controlled environment, political discourse finds a way through. This might indicate a shift in Meta's approach to managing content, potentially opening up Threads to a broader range of discussions.

However, the introduction of trending topics also brings challenges, such as ensuring the quality and relevance of what trends, managing misinformation, and dealing with potential echo chambers. Users are watching closely to see how Threads will balance the freedom of discourse with the need to maintain a safe, engaging platform. This feature's success will hinge on how well Threads can curate this list to reflect truly significant cultural or news moments.

With Threads now jumping on the trending topics bandwagon, it's like they're trying to weave together all the big conversations. But let's hope they don't get too tangled up in the web of politics. Why did the topic trend on Threads? Because it wanted to be the "thread" that everyone follows!

3. Threads Updates for 2025

Throughout 2024, Threads has undergone numerous updates aimed at enhancing user experience and engagement. Notable changes include expanding media limits, securing the threads.com domain to improve brand identity, and rolling out tests for new features like enhanced search capabilities and, most recently, trending topics. These updates signify Threads' commitment to evolving based on user feedback and competitive pressures.

One of the key focuses has been on improving how users interact with content on the platform, with updates like the ability to share posts more seamlessly across Instagram and better personalization of feeds. These changes suggest Meta is keen on making Threads not just a place for quick updates but a more comprehensive social experience where users can connect over shared interests or news.

The updates also reflect a strategic approach to compete in the crowded social media landscape. By continuously introducing new features, Threads aims to keep its user base growing while adapting to the ever-changing demands of social media users. However, each update brings its own set of challenges, including privacy concerns, user adaptation, and the overall impact on the platform's culture and community dynamics.

With all these updates, Threads is really trying to sew up the social media market. But remember, with great features come great responsibilities... like figuring out how to use them all! Why did Threads update so much? Because it didn't want to be left hanging in the social media fabric!

4. Political and Cultural Discussions on Threads

The launch of trending topics on Threads has inadvertently opened the door to political conversations, despite Meta's historical caution regarding political content. Early trends have included discussions around Donald Trump's legal battles, showcasing the platform's capability to become a significant venue for political discourse. This development could mark a pivotal moment for Threads, as it navigates the fine line between fostering open dialogue and managing the potential for misinformation or heated debates.

Cultural discussions have also found a space on Threads, with topics ranging from entertainment to social issues, reflecting the diverse interests of its user base. This blend of culture and politics has created a melting pot of conversation, where users engage with both light-hearted trends and more serious societal topics. It's a testament to the platform's growing influence in shaping public conversation, much like its predecessors in the social media space.

However, with the introduction of political content comes the challenge of moderation. Threads will need robust systems to handle the spread of misinformation, maintain civility in discussions, and perhaps most critically, ensure that all voices, particularly those from underrepresented communities, are heard. How Threads manages this influx of political and cultural discussions will be crucial for its identity and growth as a social platform.

With Threads now diving into political chats, it's like they're trying to stitch together all the hot takes. But keeping the conversation civil? That's a whole different ball of thread. Why did the politician join Threads? Because he heard it was trending to "spin" a new narrative!

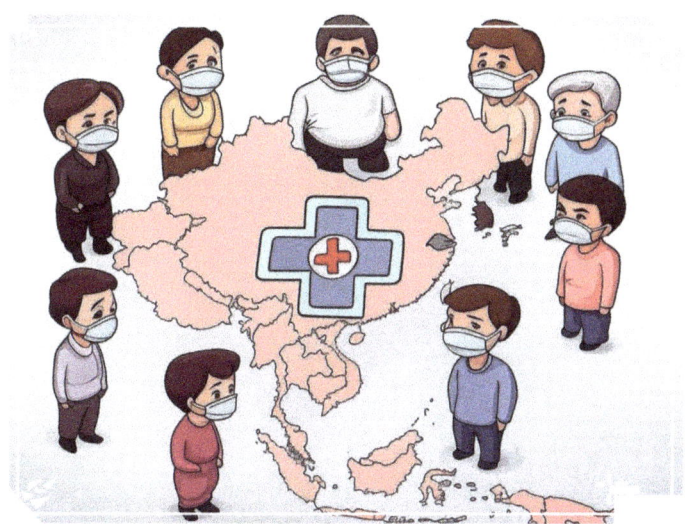

5. Health Concerns in China

The rise of Human Metapneumovirus (HMPV) in China has sparked international health concerns, particularly given the timing during the flu season. HMPV, which can cause respiratory infections, has been noted for its potential to overwhelm health systems if not monitored closely. Global health organizations are keeping a vigilant eye on the situation, sharing data and strategies to control the spread.

This situation echoes the early days of the COVID-19 outbreak, reminding the world of the importance of rapid response and international cooperation in health crises. Countries are updating their health advisories, with some considering travel restrictions or enhanced screening at airports from affected regions. The focus is not just on containment but also on understanding HMPV's behavior in a post-COVID world where health infrastructure has been tested and, in some ways, strengthened.

Public awareness campaigns have begun in earnest, aiming to educate people on symptoms, prevention measures, and the importance of not overwhelming medical facilities with non-urgent cases. The global health community is hopeful that lessons learned from previous pandemics will aid in managing this new health challenge more effectively, but the situation remains fluid, with ongoing research and monitoring to predict and mitigate further spread.

With HMPV making a splash in China, it's like the flu season decided to go viral. But don't worry, the health community is on it, trying to keep this from becoming another "pandemic sequel". Why did HMPV start trending in China? Because it wanted to be the "flu-enza" of the moment!

6. Canadian Political Landscape

The announcement of Canadian Prime Minister Justin Trudeau's resignation has sent ripples through Canadian politics and beyond. This unexpected move has led to speculation about the future direction of the Liberal Party, with many wondering who might step up to lead. Internationally, former U.S. President Donald Trump's suggestion of a merger between Canada and the U.S. has added an unusual twist to the discussion, although it's largely seen as political rhetoric.

Within Canada, the political discourse has shifted towards who will take the helm and what policies might define the next phase of Canadian governance. Trudeau's tenure was marked by progressive policies, international diplomacy, and navigating through global crises like the COVID-19 pandemic. His departure marks the end of an era, potentially opening up the field to new political ideologies or a continuation of the current path.

The idea of a U.S.-Canada merger, while not taken seriously in political circles, has sparked conversations about the relationship between the two nations, trade agreements, and border issues. It underscores the interconnectedness of North American politics and how statements from one leader can influence public discourse in another country. The coming months will be crucial in shaping Canada's political landscape as the country prepares for leadership transition.

With Trudeau stepping down, Canada's political scene is in for a shake-up. And with Trump suggesting a merger, it's like he's trying to annex Canadian politics into his next reality TV show. Why did Trudeau resign? Because he heard the only way to merge with the U.S. was to become a "politician emeritus"!

7. Viral Stories and Human Interest

One of the standout viral stories involves an Indian-origin man who used a drone to rescue a dog trapped on a cliff, showcasing not only human ingenuity but also compassion towards animals. This incident, which was shared across multiple social platforms, highlights the intersection of technology and humanitarian efforts, gaining millions of views and shares due to its feel-good factor and innovative solution to a common problem.

In another heartwarming tale, a woman in the U.S. was seen carrying a bag of Basmati rice as a fashion statement at a public event, turning an everyday grocery item into a quirky accessory. This moment of light-hearted creativity went viral, leading to discussions about fashion, cultural representation, and the often-blurred lines between utility and style. It serves as a reminder of how ordinary moments can become extraordinary when captured and shared in the right context.

Human interest stories like these not only entertain but also connect people across the globe, fostering a sense of community and shared human experience. They often carry deeper messages about kindness, innovation, or cultural identity, resonating with audiences who seek content that uplifts or educates. These stories highlight the power of social media to bring attention to acts of kindness, creativity, or simple human moments that might otherwise go unnoticed.

From drone-rescued dogs to fashionable rice bags, social media proves that sometimes, the most viral stories are the ones that warm your heart or make you laugh. Why did the dog love the drone rescue? Because it was a "bark-ting" new way to get saved!

8. Sports and Entertainment

The sports world has seen significant buzz with Sabrina Ionescu's relationship with Spike Lee being one of the trending topics. Ionescu, known for her prowess on the basketball court, has been celebrated not only for her athletic achievements but also for her cultural impact, with Lee, a renowned filmmaker and sports enthusiast, publicly supporting her. This cross-section of sports and entertainment highlights how athletes today are not just players but also cultural icons.

In the realm of cinema, Francis Ford Coppola's latest project, "Megalopolis," has been a topic of discussion due to its mixed reception at the box office. Despite the involvement of a legendary director known for classics like "The Godfather," the film's performance has sparked conversations about the changing tastes of audiences, the role of auteurs in modern cinema, and the challenges of funding and promoting experimental films.

These stories from sports and entertainment sectors illustrate the ongoing dialogue between fans, creators, and critics. They show how sports figures and filmmakers can influence cultural narratives, create trends, or even redefine what success looks like in their respective fields. The blend of sports with entertainment also reflects a broader trend where sports figures are increasingly seen as entertainers, and vice versa.

With Sabrina Ionescu teaming up with Spike Lee, it's like basketball and cinema decided to have a crossover episode. And with Coppola's "Megalopolis" stirring up the box office, it proves that even legends can't always predict the score. Why did the basketball player start hanging out with the director? Because he heard you can't spell "cinema" without "Ionescu"!

9. Social Media Trends for 2025

As we move into 2025, social media platforms like LinkedIn, Instagram, and WhatsApp have emerged as the most trusted for brand presence, signaling a shift in where businesses invest their marketing efforts. This trend reflects a move towards platforms that offer professional networking, visual storytelling, and secure communication, respectively, catering to different aspects of human interaction online.

The rise of vertical video content, driven by platforms like TikTok and Instagram Reels, continues to dominate, pushing brands and content creators to adapt their strategies to this format. This shift has also influenced how stories are told online, with a preference for quick, engaging, and visually appealing content that captures attention in seconds.

Nostalgia, particularly for the 90s and Y2K eras, has also become a significant trend in social media marketing, tapping into Gen Z's love for retro aesthetics and experiences. Brands are leveraging this by reviving old logos, bringing back classic products with modern twists, or creating content that evokes memories, thereby connecting with younger audiences through shared cultural touchstones.

In 2025, social media is all about vertical videos and 90s nostalgia, because apparently, the future is just the past standing up and looking cool. Why are brands so into vertical videos now? Because they've finally realized that the best way to capture attention is to "reel" it in!

10. Legal and Ethical Issues

Meta's founder, Mark Zuckerberg, is set to be deposed in a copyright infringement lawsuit involving the training of AI with copyrighted material. This case is one of many highlighting the ethical and legal challenges of AI development, particularly around data usage rights and privacy. The outcome of this lawsuit could set precedents for how tech companies handle intellectual property in AI training datasets.

The legal battle underscores a broader conversation about the responsibilities of tech giants in managing the vast amounts of data they process. It raises questions about ownership, consent, and compensation in the digital age, where AI's capabilities are expanding rapidly, often at the expense of individual or collective rights over content.

This situation also reflects the growing scrutiny of tech companies by both the public and regulatory bodies, focusing on how they balance innovation with ethical considerations. The implications of this lawsuit could influence future tech policies, potentially leading to stricter regulations on data use, transparency, and accountability in AI development.

With Mark Zuckerberg facing a deposition over AI training data, it's like tech companies are learning that you can't just "like" your way out of legal issues. Why did the AI go to court? Because it got caught copying homework from the internet!

11. Instagram Threads Ideas

With the introduction of Threads, there's been a surge in creative content ideas aimed at making the most of this new platform. Users are encouraged to share personal stories, engage in community discussions, and use the platform's features to create content that feels authentic and engaging. This includes using Threads for real-time reactions to events, sharing insights or daily life snippets, and fostering a space for micro-blogging.

One of the strategies for gaining traction on Threads involves leveraging Instagram's existing user base by cross-posting or linking content, ensuring a seamless transition for followers. Creators are also experimenting with different formats like polls, Q&A sessions, and educational threads to build a community around shared interests or learning.

The focus on authenticity over polished content on Threads has led to a resurgence of genuine, unfiltered interactions, which contrasts with the often curated feeds of other platforms. This approach could redefine engagement on social media, emphasizing conversation over broadcast, and personal connection over mass appeal.

Threads is all about real talk and real connections, proving that sometimes, the most engaging content is just being yourself. Why did the user start sharing on Threads? Because they heard it was the best place to "sew" together a community!

12. Global News and Events

Major global events continue to shape news cycles, with significant stories like the power grid failure in Puerto Rico causing widespread concern over infrastructure resilience and climate change impacts. This event has reignited discussions on renewable energy adoption, the need for robust disaster response systems, and international aid.

In British Columbia, stories of wildlife, particularly the interactions between bears and humans, have captured public attention, highlighting the delicate balance between urban expansion and natural habitats. These incidents serve as a reminder of the importance of wildlife conservation and human adaptation to co-exist with nature.

Global news, whether it's about natural disasters, political shifts, or environmental challenges, not only informs but also mobilizes public opinion and policy-making. These stories underline the interconnectedness of our world, where an event in one part can have ripple effects globally, prompting a collective response or action.

From power outages in Puerto Rico to bear encounters in British Columbia, it seems like Mother Nature is just trying to keep us on our toes. Or maybe she's just looking for her own social media account. Why did the bear start reading the news? Because he heard it was all about "grizzly" events!

13. Entertainment and Celebrity News

The entertainment world has been abuzz with various celebrity-related stories, including Blake Lively's lawsuit over unauthorized use of her likeness, which brings to light issues of privacy, consent, and the rights of public figures in the digital age. This case could set a precedent for how celebrities' images are used in marketing or media without explicit permission.

The passing of notable figures like John Ashton and Joe Wolf has also been a significant point of discussion, leading to tributes and reflections on their contributions to the arts and sports. These moments serve not only as a collective mourning but also as an opportunity to celebrate their legacies, influencing younger generations or those new to their work.

Celebrity news often reflects broader societal issues or trends, from legal battles over privacy to the cultural impact of artists and athletes. These stories are not just about fame but about the intersection of personal lives with public interest, legal systems, and cultural narratives.

From lawsuits over likeness to legends leaving us, the celebrity news cycle never stops spinning. It's like Hollywood drama wrote the script for real life. Why did Blake Lively sue? Because she didn't give anyone "permission" to "lively" up their marketing with her face!

14. Nostalgia and Cultural Trends

The 90s and Y2K nostalgia continues to permeate pop culture, with fashion, music, and media from these eras experiencing a revival. This trend is driven by Gen Z's fascination with a time before they were born or when they were very young, leading to a reimagining of these cultural elements through modern lenses.

From fashion runways showcasing grunge or minimalist 90s styles to the resurgence of classic video games and movies, this nostalgia wave has commercial implications, influencing marketing strategies, product design, and content creation. Brands are capitalizing on this by either reintroducing old products or creating new ones that evoke the same feelings of nostalgia.

This cultural trend also speaks to a human desire for connection to the past, offering comfort in familiar styles or stories at a time of rapid change. It's a reminder of how culture cycles through time, with each generation finding something unique to cherish or reinterpret from the past.

With 90s and Y2K vibes making a comeback, it's like we're all just trying to hit rewind on our cultural clock. Why is Gen Z so into the 90s? Because they heard the fashion was "grunge-ularly" awesome!

15. Technology and Social Media

Threads' integration with Instagram has been a strategic move by Meta to leverage its existing user base for growth. This integration allows for a seamless user experience where one can maintain their identity across platforms, share content easily, and even use Instagram to grow their Threads following. It's a testament to Meta's approach to interconnected service ecosystems.

The platform has been quick to implement user-requested features like a chronological feed, showing responsiveness to community feedback. Threads aims to differentiate itself by focusing on text-based communication in a time when visual content dominates, potentially reviving the art of conversation and storytelling in a more textual format.

However, with these advancements come privacy and data use concerns, especially given the controversies surrounding Meta's data practices. Users are keenly aware of how their information is used across these platforms, pushing for more transparency and control over their digital footprint. How Threads navigates these concerns will be crucial for its long-term success and public trust.

Threads is trying to stitch together social media by merging with Instagram, proving that in the world of tech, sharing is indeed caring. But remember, with great integration comes great privacy responsibility. Why did Threads want a chronological feed? Because it was tired of the "post" always coming before the "present"!

16. Environmental and Conservation Efforts

The National Trust's initiative to distribute saplings from a famous sycamore tree in the U.K. represents a blend of environmental conservation and cultural heritage. This project not only aims to propagate a piece of history but also to engage the public in tree planting, which is vital for climate change mitigation and biodiversity.

This effort highlights the growing trend of using cultural significance to drive environmental actions. By connecting people with nature through stories or symbols they care about, organizations can foster a stronger conservation ethic. It's also an example of how community involvement can be key to successful environmental projects.

Such initiatives reflect a broader movement towards recognizing the role of trees in combating climate change, reducing urban heat islands, and improving mental health. They also underscore the need for collaborative efforts between government, NGOs, and the public to achieve sustainable environmental outcomes.

The National Trust is planting saplings from a famous tree, blending history with green thumbs. It's like they're saying, "Let's make history grow again!" Why did the tree get into conservation? Because it wanted to make sure its "roots" were in the right place!

17. Political Dynamics

The political scene remains volatile, with events like the U.S. House's speaker election drawing significant attention. This process has highlighted internal party struggles and the broader implications for governance, as the choice of speaker can set the tone for legislative priorities and government functioning.

Internationally, political tensions, whether in the Middle East, Europe, or Asia, continue to influence global stability, trade, and diplomatic relations. These stories often reflect the complex interplay of domestic politics with international affairs, where decisions in one country can affect global markets, security, or human rights.

The coverage of these dynamics shows not just the political maneuvers but also the human stories behind them—the voters, the activists, the affected communities. It's a narrative of power, change, and sometimes, the quest for stability in an increasingly interconnected world.

From the U.S. House Speaker election to global political tensions, it's like the world's playing one big game of political chess. But remember, every move counts. Why did the politician become a chess player? Because he wanted to check-mate his way through the House!

18. Health and Wellness

The link between alcohol consumption and cancer has received renewed attention, with reports highlighting that a significant number of cases are related to drinking. This has led to public health campaigns aimed at raising awareness about moderate drinking, the risks associated with alcohol, and the benefits of reducing consumption.

Health and wellness trends are increasingly focusing on holistic approaches, where lifestyle choices like diet, exercise, and substance use are seen through the lens of long-term health outcomes. This shift in public health messaging reflects a growing understanding of how daily habits influence not just immediate well-being but also future health risks.

The conversation around alcohol and health also touches on cultural attitudes towards drinking, challenging long-held social norms in some societies and encouraging a reevaluation of what constitutes a healthy lifestyle. It's a reminder of the ongoing battle against preventable diseases through informed choices and public policy.

With all this talk about alcohol and health, it seems like the only spirits we should be lifting are at the gym. Why did the glass of wine go to the doctor? Because it heard it was on the "cancer watch" list!

19. Viral Videos and Social Media Challenges

Viral videos continue to define moments in social media culture, from the bizarre, like someone stopping fans with their tongue, to the heartwarming, like pet rescues or unexpected kindness. These videos often go beyond entertainment, providing insights into human behavior, creativity, and the power of community.

Social media challenges, whether for fun, charity, or raising awareness, can quickly spread, engaging millions in a shared activity or cause. They illustrate how social platforms can be used for good, encouraging participation that might lead to donations, increased awareness, or simply moments of joy and connection.

However, with virality comes responsibility. The impact of these videos or challenges can be profound, influencing behavior, setting trends, or even leading to dangerous copycat actions. Content creators and platforms alike must navigate the fine line between fostering community engagement and ensuring safety and ethical considerations.

From tongue-stopping fans to heartwarming rescues, social media challenges prove that virality is the new currency. But remember, with great viral power comes great responsibility. Why did the video go viral? Because it couldn't stop "fan"-ning out!

20. Sports Events and Updates

Sports continue to be a major driver of public interest, with live updates, match analyses, and athlete stories dominating discussions. Whether it's the latest soccer match in the Premier League, NBA playoff drama, or the achievements of individual athletes, sports events offer a continuous stream of content that resonates with fans worldwide.

Controversies, such as disputes over rules, player transfers, or off-field behavior, also keep the sports narrative alive, often blurring the lines between sports, entertainment, and social commentary. These stories provide not just entertainment but also a platform for discussing ethics, fairness, and the human side of sports.

The sports industry's ability to captivate audiences through both the thrill of competition and the personal stories of athletes underscores its cultural significance. Sports events are not just about the game; they're about the stories we tell through them, the lessons learned, and the communities built around shared passions.

From thrilling matches to off-field dramas, sports keep us glued to our screens, proving that life's not just about the game but the tales off the pitch too. Why did the soccer player sit on the sideline? Because he wanted to be a "spectator" of his own story!

CriticalBlast•com